This *poetry book belongs to*

....

OXFORD
UNIVERSITY PRESS

Great Clarendon Street, Oxford OX2 6DP, United Kingdom

Oxford University Press is a department of the University of Oxford.

It furthers the University's objective of excellence in research, scholarship, and education by publishing worldwide

Illustrations by: Caroline Sharpe, Alex Brychta, Sally Kilroy, Jill Newton, Judy Brown, Joe Wright, Korky Paul, Bucket, Caroline Jayne Church, Martin Ursell, Christyan Jones, Andy Cooke, Dominic Mansell, Susie Jenkin-Pearce, Valerie Petrone, Judy Brown, Peet Ellison, Rachel Ross, Graham Round, Sara-Jane Stewart, Jocelyn Wild, Valerie McBride, Frances Cony, Rachel Lockwood, Alan Marks, Jenny Williams, Meg Rutherford, Jessica Richardson-Jones, Jan Lewis.

Cover illustration by: Korky Paul

First published in 2016

British Library Cataloguing in Publication Data
Data available

978-0-19-274472-2

10 9 8 7 6 5 4 3 2

Printed in China

Paper used in the production of this book is a natural, recyclable product made from wood grown in sustainable forests.The manufacturing process conforms to the environmental regulations of the country of origin.

I Can Read! Oxford Poetry

For 7 Year Olds

With foreword by
Series Editor, John Foster

OXFORD

Acknowledgements

We are grateful to the authors in each case unless otherwise stated, for permission to include their poems:

Ann Bonner, 'The Night Visitor', first published in *Ghost Poems* (OUP, 1990), © Ann Bonner 1990, and 'Chinese Rain Dragon' first published in *Dragon Poems* (OUP, 1990), © Ann Bonner 1990.

Tony Bradman, 'I Wish I Was a Pirate', first published in *Pirate Poems* (OUP, 1991), © Tony Bradman 1991, reprinted by permission of The Agency (London) Ltd, 24 Pottery Lane, London W11 4LZ. All rights reserved.

Stanley Cook, 'The Dragon on the Wall', first published in Stanley Cook: *Come Along: Poems for Younger Children* (Huddersfield, 1978), © Stanley Cook 1978, reprinted by permission of Sarah Matthews.

Eric Finney, 'Stop Calling Me, Snow', first published in *Snow Poems* (OUP, 1990), © Eric Finney 1990, 'Pirate Chief', first published in *Pirate Poems* (OUP, 1991), 'IT', first published in *Monster Poems* (OUP, 1991), 'The Chimps', first published in *Monkey Poems* (OUP, 1991), © Eric Finney 1991, reprinted by permission of Mrs Sheilagh Finney.

John Foster, 'The Shadow Man', 'What's That?', and 'Who's Afraid?', first published in *Ghost Poems* (OUP, 1990), 'The Sick Young Dragon' and 'Storm', first published in *Dragon Poems* (OUP, 1990), 'Ten White Snowmen' and 'The Brown Bear', first published in *Snow Poems* (OUP, 1990), © John Foster 1991; 'You Little Monkey!', first published in *Monkey Poems* (OUP, 1991), and 'The Smugglers', first published in *Pirate Poems* (OUP, 1991), © John Foster 1991; with John Rice: 'Snip the Sneak', first published in *Pirate Poems* (OUP, 1991), © John Rice and John Foster 1991; with Irene Rawnsley: 'Monkey Babies', first published in *Monkey Poems* (OUP, 1991), © Irene Rawnsley and John Foster 1991.

Julie Holder, 'Corn Scratch Kwa Kwa Hen and the Fox', first published in *Fox Poems* (OUP, 1990) © Julie Holder 1990.

Martin Honeysett, 'Eating Bananas' and 'My Dad's a Gorilla', first published in *Monkey Poems* (OUP, 1991), © Martin Honeysett 1991, reprinted by permission of Penny Precious for the Estate of the author.

Jean Kenward, 'Dragon', first published in *Dragon Poems* (OUP, 1990) and 'Frozen Stiff', first published in *Snow Poems* (OUP, 1990), © Jean Kenward 1990; 'Night Light', first published in *Night Poems* (OUP, 1991) and 'Monkey', first published in *Monkey Poems* (OUP, 1991), © Jean Kenward 1991.

Judith Nicholls, 'Ghostly Lessons', first published in *Ghost Poems* (OUP, 1990) and ''No Smoking!', first published in *Dragon Poems* (OUP, 1990), © Judith Nicholls 1990; 'Pirate Song', first published in *Pirate Poems* (OUP, 1991), © Judith Nicholls 1991.

Irene Rawnsley, 'Chickaboo', first published in *Dogs Dinner* (Methuen Children's Books, 1990), © Irene Rawnsley 1990; 'The Sleepy Dragon', first published in *Dragon Poems* (OUP, 1990), © Irene Rawnsley 1990; 'Midnight Visitors', and 'Night Train', first published in *Night Poems* (OUP, 1991), © Irene Rawnsley 1991; and with John Foster 'Monkey Babies', first published in *Monkey Poems* (OUP, 1991), © Irene Rawnsley and John Foster 1991, reprinted by permission of Kate Rawnsley.

John Rice, 'Wanted: Smugglers', © John Rice 1991, and with John Foster 'Snip the Sneak', © John Rice and John Foster 1991, both first published in *Pirate Poems* (OUP, 1991).

Charles Thomson, 'Building a Dragon', first published in *Dragon Poems* (OUP, 1990), © Charles Thomson 1990; 'The Sea Monster's Snack', and 'The Lost Mermaid', first published in *Monster Poems* (OUP 1991), © Charles Thomson 1991.

Jill Townsend, 'Snowball', first published in *Snow Poems* (OUP, 1990), © Jill Townsend 1990.

Clive Webster, 'Meal-time', first published in *Monster Poems* (OUP, 1991), © Clive Webster 1991.

Although we have made every effort to trace and contact all copyright holders before publication this has not been possible in all cases. If notified, the publisher will rectify any errors or omissions at the earliest opportunity.

Welcome!

This book provides a selection of poems to share with your child, which will help them become more confident with their reading. Children whose parents read with them at home and talk about what they read have a huge advantage at school.

The National Curriculum stresses the importance of children enjoying a variety of literary forms, not just stories. This includes an emphasis on reading and understanding poetry through learning, performing and reciting it. By Year 3 children should also be able to identify themes and express views.

When you read with your child, not only do they develop their reading skills, they also learn that reading is a pleasurable activity. By reading and discussing poems together you can begin to foster an enjoyment of poetry that will extend beyond their schooldays.

As well as providing a lively collection of poems for you to share, this book contains practical tips on how to introduce the poems and suggestions of activities you can use after reading, such as how to prepare a performance.

I can remember sharing nursery rhymes and poems with my parents and with my own children. The shared experience of listening to and joining in with reciting poems is one of the reasons I started writing children's poetry. From an early age I developed an interest in the sound of words and how you could play with them to make up rhymes.

I have been lucky enough to be invited to put together collections of my own and other people's poems for you to share and enjoy with your child. I hope you will have as much fun reading and performing them together as I did choosing them.

John Foster

Contents

My Dad's a Gorilla

Do I Have to Go Haunting Tonight?

Enjoying poetry with your child

I Can Read! Oxford Poetry for 7 Year Olds is the third of three books that offer poems for parents to share and enjoy with their children. These poems are perfect for you to read aloud together with your child as they have strong **rhythms**, simple **rhyme schemes** and contain lots of repetition.

Poetry is ideal for younger readers. Your child can enjoy a feeling of success after reading a poem which is only a few pages long. Many young readers find this easier than having to read a longer book. The strong **rhythms** and **rhyme schemes** make these ideal poems for your child to learn by heart and perform. The poems in this book are a brilliant way of introducing simple literary language, using terms such as **verse**, **rhythm** and **rhyme** to discuss them. The glossary at the end of the book will help you to explain these terms, which appear in red throughout these notes.

Poetry is great for children's reading development and is a key part of the National Curriculum. These poems make ideal supplementary reading material for any child who is learning to read, so you can use them alongside storybooks such as *Read with Biff, Chip and Kipper.* You can simply read and enjoy the poems in this book together, or use the notes and tips below to help prepare your child to meet the National Curriculum requirements for poetry, which aim to develop children's ability to:

✓	Learn, recite and perform poems
✓	Listen to, read and discuss a wide range of poems
✓	Recognise simple literary language and use terms such as **verse, rhythm** and **rhyme**
✓	Show an understanding of poems while reading aloud through **intonation**, volume and action.

Tips and Ideas for developing reading skills

Introducing literary language

★ Discuss how bears hibernate in the winter and read **The Brown Bear** (p. 20). Talk about how the poem is in two halves, the first half describing the winter cold and the second half describing the bear's dreams of summer heat. Point out to your child how the poet uses repetition, **rhyme** and **alliteration**.

★ Read **Night Train** (p. 92) and talk about how the train is compared to a caterpillar. Explain that this is a **metaphor**. Ask your child if they think it is an effective comparison? Can they suggest something else the train might be compared to, such as a worm or a snake? Work together to draft a similar poem in which the night train is compared to a snake or other creature.

★ Talk about what happens to the washing if you put it out on a frosty day, then read **Frozen Stiff** (p. 22). Explain what a **simile** is and point out how the poet uses comparisons to say how stiff and hard the clothes are. Talk about how she describes the clothes clinging to the line. Recite the poem, **emphasising** the **rhythm** to express the child's amazement at how frozen the clothes are.

★ Ask your child what it might be like to throw snowballs or to be hit by one. Then read **Snowball** (p. 24) and find the comparisons that the poet makes, discussing why they are **metaphors**.

> **TOP TIP!** Read the other poems in ***Stop Calling Me, Snow*** and look out for examples that will help illustrate the literary terms above, as well as others such as **verse**, **narrator**, **fable**, **rhythm** and wordplay.

Recognising rhyme and rhythm

★ Share **Pirate Chief** (p. 28). Discuss the pattern of the poem and how it is written in **couplets** which give it a jaunty **rhythm**. Encourage your child to read it in a bossy way, **emphasising** the **rhythm**.

★ Show your child the picture illustrating **I Wish I Was a Pirate** (p. 26) and talk about the typical features of a pirate that it shows. Then read the poem and talk about why the person wants to be a pirate. Draw attention to the pattern of the poem and then re-read the poem, **emphasising** its **rhythm**.

★ Read and discuss **Snip the Sneak** (p. 32). Why is the boy keen to become a smuggler and what does he think would make a good smuggler? Point out that it has the same **verse** pattern as **Mealtime** (p. 36) and **Who's Ugly?** (p. 40) Encourage your child to read the poems to you.

★ Read **What's That?** (p. 88) to your child. Draw attention to the pattern of the poem as a series of questions and answers. Discuss who is asking the questions and who is giving the answers. Point out how the child is worried and frightened by the sounds and how the parent answers reassuringly. Re-read the poem with your child asking the questions fearfully and you providing the answers confidently and reassuringly.

> **TOP TIP!** Read the other poems in *Yo-Ho-Ho! We're Off to Sea!* to find one that has a strong **rhythm**. Help your child to learn to chant the poem with you, using the repetition and the **rhymes** as prompts.

Discussing and comparing poems

★ Share **St George and the Dragon** (p. 50) and **No Smoking!** (p. 60) Make sure your child knows the legend of St George. Then read the poem and talk about how the dragon behaves differently from how St George expected it to behave. Ask how the dragon in **No Smoking!** behaves differently from the way you would expect a dragon to behave. Which of the poems does your child prefer and why?

★ Read the three poems **Dragon** (p. 56), **The Sleepy Dragon** (p. 48) and **The Dragon on the Wall** (p. 54). Encourage your child to compare the poems. How are they similar and how are they different? Point out that **Dragon** tells a story, while the other two poems are more descriptive. Discuss which poem gives the most detailed description of the dragon. Compare the style of the poems. Which poem has the strongest **rhythm**? Encourage your child to read the poems aloud and to discuss which is the most effective when read aloud.

★ Read **Storm** (p. 59). Discuss how in the first **verse** the poet suggests that the dragon is responsible for the storm and together suggest other creatures that could be responsible, such as a giant or a herd of elephants. Work together to draft another **verse**, for example: 'A herd of elephants / stampedes across the sky. / Lightning flashes. Thunder booms / The clouds begin to cry.'

★ Discuss how **Midnight Visitors** (p. 80) consists of four descriptions of how nocturnal animals move and ask your child which description they think creates the best picture. Encourage them to pick out the words and phrases the poet uses to create that picture.

> **TOP TIP!** Children are required by the National Curriculum to identify **themes** in the poems and stories they read. Share the other poems in *Panting Flames and Sneezing Sparks* looking for **themes**. Do any of the poems have similar **themes**?

Performing poems

★ Read **Chickaboo** (p. 66) and discuss what happens in the story. Then re-read the poem, with you as the **narrator** and your child speaking what is said by Chickaboo, the tree and the sun. Encourage them to use different voices for the different characters – Chickaboo all eager to play, the tree expressing concern and trying to stop Chickaboo climbing further and the sun laughingly saying that it's far too busy to play.

★ Read **You Little Monkey**! (p. 70) and talk about the way the girl behaves and how her mum teaches her a lesson. Encourage your child to recite the poem, **emphasising** the contrast between how the child feels when she is pretending to be a monkey and how she feels when she is only given monkey food for her tea.

★ Read **When You Talk to a Monkey** (p. 64) and **Eating Bananas** (p. 65). Ask your child which of these two poems they like the most and why. Talk about the actions you could make when performing **When You Talk to a Monkey**. Can they suggest actions to make while performing **Eating Bananas**? Encourage them to learn the poems and to perform the actions as they recite them.

★ Talk about how scary it can be if the light bulb on the landing breaks and you have to go upstairs in the dark. Then read **The Shadow Man** (p. 76) and invite your child to develop a performance of the poem. Discuss how to read the poem using your voice to suggest fear and reading the **verses** slowly and with pauses between them. Encourage your child to experiment with different ways of saying the last line. Which do they think works best – saying it in a loud voice or whispering it softly?

> **TOP TIP!** Choose another poem from *My Dad's a Gorilla* for your child to learn off by heart. Discuss how they could enhance the performance by using different voices or **intonation**, or by adding actions.

Stop Calling Me, Snow

Look for other poetry collections that you can share with your child, such as **Don't Eat Soup with Your Fingers** *and* **When Dad Scored a Goal in the Garden**. *As you read them, look out for examples of literary devices such as* **similes**, **metaphors** *and* **alliteration**.

Who Saw the Footprints in the Snow?

Who saw the footprints in the snow?
Who came along and where did she go?

The farmer's wife has just been out
To scatter bits of bread about.

Who saw the footprints in the snow?
Who came along and where did he go?

One little sparrow was out today,
He ate some bread and hopped away.

Who saw the footprints in the snow?
Who came along and where did she go?

A pigeon ate some breadcrumbs too,
She walked around, then off she flew.

A cat crept up behind the hedge,
Then sprang onto the window ledge.

Who saw the footprints in the snow?
Who came along and where did she go?

A squirrel found the snow too deep,
So went off home to have some sleep.

On his horse, the farmer's son
Went riding off to have some fun.

Anon

Stop Calling Me, Snow

Stop calling me, snow,
I can't come just yet,
I've got ten sums to do
That the teacher just set.

So it's no good you flapping
Your downy white wings,
It's half an hour yet
Till the playtime bell rings.

Some kids will stay in,
But not me – no fear!
I'll dive straignt for my wellies –
I can see them from here.

And I might build a snowman,
Or perhaps a snow queen,
Or I might just tread prints
Where nobody's been;

Then an igloo maybe,
With a tunnel to crawl,
Or perhaps I'll roll up
A monster snowball.

I'll stand in the whirl of your flakes
Till I'm dizzy.
But I can't come just yet –
I'm supposed to be busy . . .

There's this sum: 'Find
A half of a half.' I don't know . . .
I simply can't think . . .
Stop calling me, snow!

Eric Finney

Ten White Snowmen

Ten white snowmen standing in a line,
One toppled over, then there were nine.

Nine white snowmen standing up straight,
One lost his balance, then there were eight.

Eight white snowmen in a snowy heaven,
The wind blew one over, then there were seven.

Seven white snowmen with pipes made of sticks,
One slumped to the ground, then there were six.

Six white snowmen standing by the drive,
One got knocked down, then there were five.

Five white snowmen outside the front door,
An icicle fell on one, then there were four.

Four white snowmen standing by the tree,
One slipped and fell apart, then there were three.

Three white snowmen underneath the yew,
One crumbled overnight, then there were two.

Two white snowmen standing in the sun,
One melted right down, then there was one.

One white snowman standing all alone,
Vanished without a trace, then there were none.

John Foster

The Brown Bear

In winter,
When the cold winds blow,
When the land
Is covered with snow,
The brown bear sleeps.

In winter,
When the nights come soon,
When the land
Freezes beneath the moon
The brown bear dreams.

The brown bear
Dreams of summer heat,
Of berries,
Honey and nuts to eat.
The brown bear sighs.

The brown bear
Stirs, then digs down deep,
Safe and sound
In its winter sleep.
The brown bear dreams.

John Foster

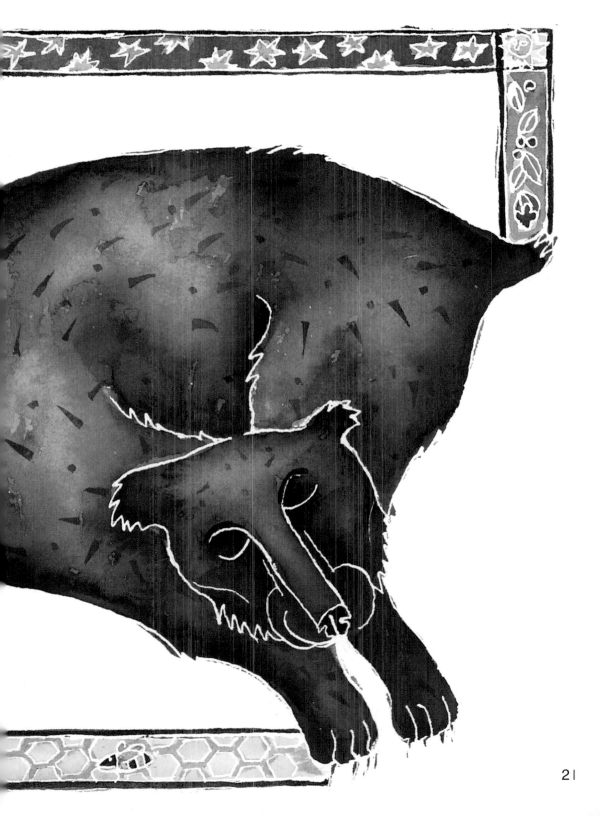

Frozen Stiff

Stiff as a battleship
prim as a pin
look at the washing;
the frost is in!

Nighties, pyjamas
and petticoats too –
hard as the buckle
upon my shoe.

Punch them and pull them.
They won't let go
of the long clothes line
for they love it so.

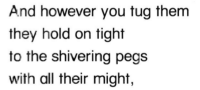

And however you tug them
they hold on tight
to the shivering pegs
with all their might,

As if they would cry
'Oh, leave us please!
We love to hang here
and freeze and freeze!'

Look at my trousers,
there's ice on the hem!
I shan't sit down
when I'm wearing them!

Jean Kenward

Snowball

Mine is a comet
whistling through space
toward a distant planet.
But the planet is a head
in a woolly hat,
and my snowball misses it.

Jill Townsend

24

Yo-Ho-Ho! We're Off to Sea!

Play rhyming games, such as **rhyme** tennis, in which you and your child take it in turns to think of rhyming words. For example, you start with the word 'ball', your child replies 'wall' and you go on exchanging words until one of you is stuck. The other person wins a point.

I Wish I Was a Pirate

I wish I was a pirate
With a long beard hanging down,
A cutlass dangling from my belt,
My teeth all black and brown.

A parrot on my shoulder.
A patch upon one eye,
A pirate ship to sail on,
A pirate flag to fly.

The rolling waves would be my home,
I'd live through many wrecks.
I'd always have the best of maps –
The ones marked with an X!

Pirates don't have parents,
They don't get sent to school.
They never have to take a bath,
For them there are no rules.

Yo-ho-ho me hearties!
It's a pirate's life for me . . .
Pistols in my pockets,
Salt-pork with my tea!

Tony Bradman

Pirate Chief

'I'm Blackbeard, boss of this pirate crew.
Now let's see about the rest of you . . .
Sue, you can be One Eye, my trusty mate,
And you're in charge of the portholes, Kate.
And you'll do all the cooking, Sally,
Slaving away in the greasy galley.
We'll all set sail from the port of Bristol,
I'll have a cutlass and a pistol;
You'll all have daggers, sharp and bright,
And it's Spanish gold we're after, right?
Zoe, you're just an ordinary pirate:
You'll polish the cannon and maybe fire it.
Nazreen and Lina: you'll swab decks.
Think of islands, palm trees, treasure, wrecks!
I just can't wait to put out to sea . . .'

'That's all very well. What about me?'

'I hadn't forgotten about you, Frank.
I've got you down to walk the plank.'

Eric Finney

Pirate Song

Yo-ho-ho, we're off to sea!
Hoist the skull and bones!
The wild waves pull,
the sails are full,
the wind in the rigging moans.

Silk and satin, silver, gold;
fill up the cabins,
fill up the hold!
With a YO-HO-HO
the wild waves roll.

Yo-ho-ho, we're off to sea
to search for silk and gold!
The wild waves pull,
the sails are full,
the wind in the rigging cold.

Silk and satin, silver, gold;
fill up the cabins,
fill up the hold!
With a YO-HO-HO
the wild waves roll.

Yo-ho-ho, we're off to sea
under the stars and moon!
The wild waves pull,
the sails are full,
the wind will take us soon.

Silk and satin, silver, gold;
fill up the cabins,
fill up the hold!
With a YO-HO-HO
the wild waves roll.

Yo-ho-ho, we're off to sea,
racing under the cloud!
The wild waves pull,
the sails are full,
the wind howls long and loud.

Silk and satin, silver, gold;
fill up the cabins,
fill up the hold!
With a YO-HO-HO
the wild waves roll.

Yo-ho-ho, we're off to sea
to sail in the wild wind's roar.
The wild waves pull,
the sails are full;
may the wind blow us back to shore!

Silk and satin, silver, gold;
fill up the cabins,
fill up the hold!
With a YO-HO-HO
the wild waves roll.

Judith Nicholls

Snip the Sneak

I'm reading a book about smugglers
And the exciting things they did,
About the goods that they smuggled
And the caves in which they hid.

I think I'd be a good smuggler
For I could sneak in and out,
I could sneak up and sneak down,
I could creep and crawl about.

I'm going to look in the papers
Where they advertise each week.
I'm going to become a smuggler.
I'll be known as Snip the Sneak.

John Rice and John Foster

WANTED... SMUGGLERS

No experience necessary. Long trips abroad.
No pets (except parrots). Excellent money to
be made. Applicants must not be afraid of
customs men or high waves.
Apply on parchment to
Jack "The Keg" Kingston
The Hawkhurst Gang
near the beach
Kent.

Smugglers

This morning,
While Mum was having a lie-in,
Because it's Saturday,
My sister and I
Emptied our money boxes
And went down town
To buy the scarf
We know she'll like.

When we got home,
My sister went in first
And kept her talking,
While I smuggled the scarf upstairs
And hid it in the shoebox
Under my bed.

Tonight,
We'll write the cards
We smuggled in
Earlier in the week
And wrap up the scarf.

Then, in the morning,
We'll give ourselves up,
Hand over the smuggled goods
And watch Mum's face
As she opens her presents
On Mother's Day.

John Foster

Mealtime

The octopus has got eight arms,
And I just cannot see
Which ones he uses to eat food
When he sits down to tea.

Does he have four knives and forks?
It really is amusing.
I wonder how he hits his mouth –
It must be quite confusing.

Clive Webster

The Sea Serpent

A sea serpent saw a big tanker,
Bit a hole in her side and then sank her.
It swallowed the crew
In a minute or two,
And then picked its teeth with the anchor.

Anon

IT

It was huge,
It was enormous,
It came dripping from the sea;
It wobbled down the promenade,
It passed quite close to me!

It ruined all the flower beds,
It upset an ice-cream stall,
It was like a giant jellyfish and
It had no eyes at all.

It cleared the paddling pool of kids,
Its feelers swung and swayed,
It seemed to like the fruit machines as
It oozed through the arcade.

It burst the turnstile on the pier as
It squeezed its green mass through,
It left a horrid track behind –
It was like a trail of glue.

It reached the pier's end railings and
It forced them till they split.
If flopped back down into the sea and
It vanished. That was it.

Eric Finney

39

Who's Ugly?

The monster was big, he was ugly,
He lived in the deeps of the sea.
He had three different eyes, but only one ear,
And a mouth where his chin ought to be.

He was covered with seaweed and shells
But he wasn't too bothered with those.
He had twenty-two legs, twenty-two feet,
And a bump on the end of his nose.

It's quite sad to say he was made in this way,
For this monster was loving and kind.
And when fish in the sea went out for their tea
They left him their babies to mind.

There's a moral, of course, to this story,
So remember, for what it is worth,
That your goldfish might think when you watch him,
That you're the ugliest person on earth.

Finola Akister

The Sea Monster's Snack

Deep down upon his sandy bed
the monster turned his slimy head,
grinned and licked his salty lips
and ate another bag of ships.

Charles Thomson

The Lost Mermaid

A mermaid came out of the plughole
And said with a frown, 'Excuse me,
I think I have made a wrong turning.
Is this a cave in the sea?'

Charles Thomson

Panting Flames
and
Sneezing Sparks

Encourage your child to draft and write poems with you. For example, you can follow the instructions on how to write nonsense nursery rhymes, riddles and chants in the Oxford Children's Rhyming Dictionary. Ask your child to illustrate the poems and then create your own poetry book.

The Sick Young Dragon

'What can I do?' Young Dragon cried.
'Although I've really tried and tried,
It doesn't matter how hard I blow,
I cannot get my fire to go!'

'Open your mouth!' his mother said.
'It's no wonder! Your throat's not red.
Your scales are cold. You must be ill.
I think you must have caught a chill.'

The doctor came. He looked and said,
'You need a day or two in bed.
Your temperature's down. That's why
Your fire's gone out and your throat's dry.

'Just drink this petrol. Chew these nails.
They'll help you to warm up your scales.
Just take it easy. Watch TV.
You'll soon be well again, you'll see.'

Young dragon did as he was told
And soon his scales stopped feeling cold.
He sneezed some sparks. His face glowed bright.
He coughed and set the sheets alight.

'Oh dear!' he cried. 'I've burnt the bed!'
'It doesn't matter,' his mother said.
'Those sheets were old. Go out and play.
Just watch where you breathe fire today!'

John Foster

The Sleepy Dragon

A dragon awoke
in his mountain lair
where he'd slept
for a thousand years.

His treasure was rusty
his scales were dusty
his throat was dry
his wings wouldn't fly
his throat was croaky
his fire was smoky
his eyes weren't flashing
his tail wasn't lashing
his claws couldn't scratch
though he tried.

So he sighed
and stretched himself
over the floor
and went back to sleep
for a thousand years more.

Irene Rawnsley

49

St George and the Dragon

St George looked at the dragon
And much to his surprise,
He noticed that the dragon
Had large, appealing eyes.
'Pardon me,' said brave St George,
'I hear you're cruel and sly.'
'Oh no, not me,' the dragon said,
'I wouldn't hurt a fly.'
'I've come to slay you,' said St George,
'And save the maiden fair
That you have captured, and no doubt
Imprisoned in your lair.'
'I used to be cruel and sly,
Of that there is no doubt,'
Replied the dragon, 'but not now,
My fire has all burnt out.
The maiden you have come to save
Has made a pet of me.
She takes me walkies on a lead
And feeds me cups of tea.
So if you want to do brave deeds
The like of which I've read,
Please take the maiden home with you,
And so save me instead.'

Finola Akister

50

Building a Dragon

Once I built a dragon
Three times the size of you.
I made him out of cardboard
and chicken wire and glue.

It took me weeks and weeks and weeks
until I got him right.
I hid him in the loft by day
and worked on him at night.

The cardboard came from boxes
I asked the grocer for.
I borrowed tins of paint
from Mr Brown next door.

It took me weeks and weeks and weeks
(well, four at least – no, five!)
and then I got a nasty shock:
the dragon came alive.

It burst out through the roof –
so I could see the stars –
went crashing down the road
and damaged several cars.

I've looked for him for weeks and weeks.
Where did my dragon go?
If anyone has seen him, will
they kindly let me know?

Charles Thomson

The Dragon on the Wall

A bright green dragon comes in through the door
And crawls along the classroom wall.
He must be lost
Or need a rest,
For he never came into the classroom before.

His body is covered with rough nobbly scales.
He could pull down a tree that he hooked with his tail.
He rests on the wall, his mouth open wide,
Puffing and panting flames from inside.

His green silky wings are raised on his back,
Ready to give a mighty great flap.
He perches beside the open window
As if he is waiting for us to go.

When we leave him on his own
Does he fly home
In a streak of light
Through the black of the night
To see that his cave is safe
With all its bright shining gold?

Stanley Cook

Dragon

There was a dragon
    came to tea
        and ate
            a currant bun.

He said it was
    so tasty, that
        he'd try another
            one!

He ate the treacle
    sandwiches.
        He ate the lemon
            cake . . .

He ate a dish
    of flapjacks – more
        than anyone
            should take.

He nibbled all
    the tiny things
        and swallowed down
            the great ones,

He fr ghtened all
    the early guests,
        and hurried off
            the late ones.

He cleared the biscuits
    from the tin –
        he never left
            a crumb.

If he is ever
    asked again,
        I hope **HE WILL NOT
            COME**!

Jean Kenward

57

Chinese Rain Dragon

Dance, Dragon, dance.
Make the rain come.
Dance, Dragon, dance.
Banish the sun.

Dance, Dragon, dance.
Beat on the drum.
Try, Dragon, try,
To make the rain come.

The earth is dry, Dragon.
Crops will die, Dragon.
Bring dark sky, Dragon.
Oh when will it come?

Try once again, Dragon.
Here comes the rain, Dragon!
You have won, Dragon.
Dragon! Well done!

Ann Bonner

Storm

The sky is full of dragon light.
The forks of lightning flash.
The sky is full of dragon roars.
The rolls of thunder crash.

The dark clouds race across the sky.
Down comes the pouring rain.
The green shoots burst out of the earth.
The farmer smiles again.

John Foster

59

No Smoking!

Blow us a bonfire, dragon,
light up the sky!
But the dragon blushed
to his scaly tail
as he whispered,
>   *'I'm shy!'*

Give us a puff please, dragon,
just *one* small huff!
But the dragon paled
to his scaly tail
and he whispered,
>   *'I'm not tough!'*

Show us some smoke then, dragon,
blow us some now!
But the dragon's head
turned three shades of red
and he whispered,
>   *'I don't know how!'*

Judith Nicholls

My Dad's a Gorilla

Look for clues in the poem that can provide ideas about how to perform them. For example, you could look for examples of **onomatopoeia** or words that describe a character's mood, or words that describe sounds and actions.

The Chimps

Oh, the lions were growly,
The tigers were prowly,
The zebras kept quietly grazing;
Kangaroos were all jumpy
And camels were humpy –
But the chimps were really amazing!

We heard rattlesnakes rattle,
Saw huge, hairy cattle
And lobsters and land crabs and shrimps.
There were penguins like waiters
And great alligators –
But we kept going back to the chimps.

There were dolphins and seals,
A stingray, some eels
And polar bears white as the snow,
But the chimps were our aces:
Their habits and faces
Were just like some people we know!

Eric Finney

63

When You Talk to a Monkey

When you talk to a monkey
    He seems very wise.
He scratches his head,
    And he blinks both his eyes;
But he won't say a word.
    He just swings on a rail
And makes a big question mark
    Out of his tail.

Rowena Bennett

Eating Bananas

'Bananas,' said the monkey,
'Are what I like to eat,
And if my hands are busy
I peel them with my feet.'

Martin Honeysett

Chickaboo

Chickaboo monkey
lived in the jungle;
climbed to the top
of a very tall tree.

Looked at the sky,
a big blue blanket;
looked at the leaves,
a big green sea;

looked at the sun,
a big orange ball
and said,

'I want the sun to play with!'

The tree shook its branches;
'No, no, no;
you've climbed as high
as a monkey can go.'

But Chickaboo
jumped high
and higher
and higher than high
till he rolled on the blanket
of the big blue sky.

He rolled to the ball
of the golden sun
and said,

'I've come to play with you.'

But the sun said,
'I've no time to play;
I'm much too busy
making day.'

Then the sun stuck out
his golden tongue
and sent little Chickaboo
rolling home.

Irene Rawnsley

Tale of the Clever Monkey

Two cats were fighting
over a ship's biscuit.
Miaaow! Spitt! Miaaow!
Along came a clever monkey.
'Have half each,' he said.

He broke the biscuit
but it was unequal.
'Oh dear,' said the monkey.
The cats started fighting again.
Miaaow! Spitt! Miaaow!

'Wait! I'll nibble a bit
so you'll have the same each,'
said the clever monkey.
But he nibbled *too much*.
The pieces were *still* unequal.

Miaaow! Spitt! Miaaow!
'Hey, stop fighting!'
said the clever monkey.
And he nibbled a bit more
of the ship's biscuit.

The pieces were *still* unequal
so the clever monkey
nibbled and nibbled until
the whole biscuit had gone!
'Um, that *was* good!' he said.

The cats started fighting again.
Miaaow! Spitt! Miaaow!
The clever monkey
licked his lips
and ran away . . . laughing.

Wes Magee

You Little Monkey!

My mum said
I was behaving
like a little monkey.

So I climbed
onto the sofa
and started swinging
on the door.

When she told me to stop,
I made chattering noises
and pretended
to scratch my armpits.

I refused
to talk properly
until lunchtime,
when all I got
was a plate of nuts
and a banana!

So I decided
to stop
monkeying around.

John Foster

My Dad's a Gorilla

My dad's a gorilla when he gets mad,
He starts to rant and roar.
Then walks about on his hands and knees,
And rolls around the floor.
He's also very hairy,
Hairs poke out through his vest,
And like a real gorilla
He stands and thumps his chest.

Martin Honeysett

Monkey Babies

Don't leave your monkey baby
sitting by the swamp;
a crocodile might eat him.
Chomp! Chomp! Chomp!

Don't leave your monkey baby
sitting under the trees;
a snake might wrap him up.
Squeeze! Squeeze! Squeeze!

Don't leave your monkey baby
sitting by the track;
a lion might be lurking.
Snack! Snack! Snack!

Keep your monkey baby
high up in the trees.
Feed him on bananas.
Help pick off his fleas.

Irene Rawnsley and John Foster

Monkey

His eyes are sad.
He nibbles a banana
and looks at me
between the iron bars.

We are so close.
But he is in a prison
that seems as far
as Jupiter or Mars.

What does he dream of
when the darkness thickens
and all the eager visitors
are gone?

The green, deep forest,
where for years and years
monkeys have played and tumbled
in the sun.

Jean Kenward

Do I Have to Go Haunting Tonight?

Before you read a poem, talk about its title. Ask your child if the title suggests what the poem is going to be about. Similarly, does the illustration offer any clues? Encourage your child to look for other poems about ghosts, dragons and pirates in poetry collections in the library, such as John Foster and Korky Paul's **Dragon Poems.**

The Shadow Man

At night-time
As I climb the stair
I tell myself
There's nobody there.

But what if there is?
What if he's there –
The Shadow Man
At the top of the stair?

What if he's lurking
There in the gloom
Of the landing
Right outside my room?

The Shadow Man
Who's so hard to see
What if he's up there
Waiting for me?

At night-time
As I climb the stair
I tell myself
There's nobody there.

John Foster

Night Light

Can I have a night light?
Yes, of course you can.
I'll put it on
the landing
to beat the Bogeyman.

He doesn't like a bright light.
He doesn't like the glare.
It swallows up
the darkness
and shows he isn't there.

You can have a night light
burning bright and strong
to drive away
the darkness
all night long.

Jean Kenward

Midnight Visitors

Hedgehog comes snuffing
in his prickly coat,
scuffing the leaves for slugs.

Cat comes soft as a moth,
a shadow painted on the lawn
by moonlight.

Owl comes floating,
sits still as a cat on the wall,
watching, listening.

Mouse freezes under the leaves
on tiptoe paws,
quick eyes pin-bright,
hungry.

Irene Rawnsley

The Corn Scratch Kwa Kwa Hen and the Fox

And the Corn Scratch Kwa Kwa Hen
Heard the grumbling rumbling belly
Of the Slink Back Brush Tail Fox
A whole field away.

And she said to her sisters in the henhouse,
'Sisters, that Slink Back Brush Tail Fox
Will come and here's what we must do,'
And she whispered in their sharp sharp ears, 'kwa kwa.'

And when that Slink Back Brush Tail Fox
Came over the field at night,
She heard his paw slide on a leaf,
And the Corn Scratch Kwa Kwa Hen and her sisters
Opened their beaks and –

'KWA!'
The moon jumped
And the Chooky Chook Chicks
Hid under the straw and giggled.
It was the **LOUDEST KWA** in the world.

And the Log Dog and the Scat Cat
And the Brat Rat and the House Mouse
And the Don't Harm Her Farmer
And his Life Wife and their Shorter Daughter
And their One Son came running,

On their slip slop, flip flop,
Scatter clatter, slick flick, tickly feet
And they opened their mouths and shouted –

'FOX!'
And it was the **LOUDEST NAME** in the world.
And the Slick Back Brush Tail Fox
Ran over the fields and far away
And hid in a hole with his grumbling rumbling belly.

And the Corn Scratch Kwa Kwa Hen
Tucked the Chooky Chook Chicks under her feathers
And said, 'kwa,'
And it was the softest kwa in the world.

Julie Holder

The Night Visitor

Some
THING
went
bump
in the
night.

THUMP
in the
night.
Gave
me a
fright.

A shadow
moved
on the
wall.
Long-
legged
and
terribly
tall.

A ghoulie?
Or
ghostie
in white?
A trick
of the
light?

No.
Nothing
went
bump
but that
BEASTLY

lump
of a
cat.
Asleep!
On my
bed.

She
made me
jump
last night.

Ann Bonner

87

What's That?

What's that rustling at the window?
Only the curtain flapping in the breeze.

What's that groaning in the garden?
Only the branches swaying in the trees.

What's that rattling at the front door?
Only the wind in the letter-box flap.

What's that drumming in the bathroom?
Only the dripping of the leaking tap.

What's that hissing in the front room?
Only the gas as it burns in the fire.

What's that murmur in the kitchen?
Only the whirring of the tumble dryer.

What's that shadow lurking
    in the corner beside the door?
It's only your clothes where you left them
    lying on the bedroom floor.

John Foster

Ghostly Lessons

Mum, I want some chocolate,
just one little treat –
peppermint or strawberry cream . . .
GHOSTS DON'T EAT!

Mum, I've got a toothache,
a pain beneath my heel;
my throat's too sore to work tonight . . .
GHOSTS DON'T FEEL!

Mum, I really hate the dark –
I hate the way they stared!
I'm scared of graveyards, woods and folk . . .
GHOSTS AREN'T SCARED!

Judith Nicholls

Who's Afraid?

Do I have to go haunting tonight?
The children might give me a fright.
It's dark in that house.
I might meet a mouse.
Do I have to go haunting tonight?

I don't like the way they scream out,
When they see me drifting about.
I'd much rather stay here,
Where there's nothing to fear.
Do I have to go haunting tonight?

John Foster

Night Train

The train
is a shiny caterpillar
in clackety boots
nosing through the blind night,
munching mile after mile
of darkness.

Irene Rawnsley

Glossary

alliteration the use of several closely connected words which begin with the same letter or sound, e.g. slip, slop. slap

couplet a pair of lines ending with words that rhyme

emphasise to put stress on a word or words

fable a short story ending with a moral

intonation varying the pitch of your voice, making it rise or fall in order to convey emotion or meaning

metaphor a phrase comparing one thing to another without the use of 'like' or 'as', for example 'The train / is a giant caterpillar'.

narrator the person or character who is telling a story

onomatopoeia the use of a word or phrase which has a sound that echoes its meaning, e.g. hiss, buzz, clatter

rhyme words which end with the same sound or sounds are said to make a rhyme

rhyme scheme the pattern of rhymes in a poem

rhythm the flow of words or phrases in a poem, based on the number and type of syllables they have

riddle a word puzzle in which you write about something without saying what it is, so that the reader must use the clues to work it out

simile comparing one thing with another by using 'like' or 'as', e.g. 'as big as an elephant'

theme the subject of a poem, or an idea such as friendship or celebration which runs throughout the poem

verse a section of a poem, often with the same rhyme scheme as other sections

Index of First Lines